for

Don't Sweat It, Kid

2nd Edition

This book belongs to

Brianna Frink

Is this a gift?

☐   no

☒   yes

From: *Uncle Carroll & Aunt Venny*

Author's Signature

Dr. Jayce Teal

Date *1-25-16*

Dedication

For my beautiful niece, Sandra,

her handsome husband, Gary,

and their lovely daughters, Brieanna

and Brittany.

You are so special, and I am

immensely proud of you!

Don't Sweat It, Kid

2nd Edition

Don't Sweat It,
Kid…

It's not really important
in the grand scheme
of things.

Trust me on this!

❖

Knowledge can make a powerful
difference
in how you view your world!

Acknowledgements

I would like to acknowledge the
following people
for assisting in the creation of this work:

My husband, Prince O. Teal, who is
always willing
to be my sounding board

*My beautiful, intelligent nieces: Brienna,
Courtney, Brittany, and Krystal – who know*

what the  is!

Table of Contents
Volume 1

Dedication

For the Young Reader

Don't Sweat It, Kid

Don't Sweat It, Kid is a three-volume set of books that consists of more 100 topics relevant to the lives of young people in sixth through twelfth grades (and possibly beyond). These topics have been included in the three volumes because young people in these age groups have expressed the desire for a reference to which they can refer to learn more about these topics.

The author hopes that the topics discussed here will help parents and their children engage in discussions together. As a classroom teacher of many years, the author knows that these topics can assist to open and/or improve the lines of communication between parents and children as well as counselors/youth directors and their clients. They can also help children to better cope with trying situations and thus, the primary objectives of these volumes.

Finally, young people are invited to e-mail additional topics of interest to the author for inclusion in a future volume which she promises to write if there is adequate interest. To this end, children and parents are invited to read the volumes together and to decide about additional topics that would be helpful. E-mail them to joycewteal@gmail.com

Just a few of the topics you can read about in this book are:
-Bullying
-Drugs
-Social Media/Social Networking
-Don't Text While Driving

-Positive Attitude
-Making Friends

This book consists of the first 33 of the 101 topics. *Hang In There, Kid* (Volume 2), available on Amazon Kindle, consists of topics 34 through 65. *Just Do It, Kid* (Volume 3), available on Amazon Kindle, consists of topics 66 through 101. These 101 topics have been chosen because of their relevance to your life and the lives of other young people just like you. Read it with an open mind. Share it with a friend. It has the potential to help you to become a better person, a more giving and forgiving family member and a wonderful role model for the younger children who are part of your world.

Introduction

Don't Sweat It, Kid consists of three volumes that are loaded with information and scenarios that are designed to provoke thought and effect positive changes in your behavior and way of thinking about ordinary occurrences and experiences in your life. You'll find easy solutions to some of your most recurring problems and stress-provoking situations.

As a young person entering or going through adolescence, there have been or will be times during this phase of your life when you will have to make decisions that can potentially change or set the course for the rest of your life. *Don't Sweat It, Kid* has been written for you. It can help you to make these important decisions, and it can help you to make them in a way that will be advantageous to you.

This book consists of the first 33 of 100 topics. *Hang In There, Kid* (Volume 2) consists of topics 34 through 65, and *Just Do It, Kid* (Volume 3) consists of topics 66 through 100. These 100 topics have been chosen because of their pertinence to your life and the lives of other young people just like you.

Read it with an open mind. Share it with a friend. It has the potential to help you to become a better person, a more giving and forgiving family member and a wonderful role model for the younger kids who are part of your world.

If there is adequate response to this idea, perhaps I'll write a fourth volume of the **Don't Sweat It, Kid** series. If you like, you can e-mail them to: joycewteal@gmail.com

1.

Don`t Sweat It, Kid

Think about how much easier your life could be, and how much happier you could be, if you learned not to sweat the small stuff, and that most, if not all of it, is small stuff. For example, suppose you go into the cafeteria at school today and another group of students is sitting at the table where you and your friends have sat since school started this year.

As you enter the cafeteria and observe these other kids sitting at *your table*, you immediately look around for your buddies. You spot three of them in the fast food line. You walk over to them and just as you are about to ask them if they see who's sitting at *your table*, one of the cafeteria monitors, a teacher who you already don't like says, "Go to the end of the line. You know cutting isn't allowed."

You then tell him, "I'm not trying to cut. I'm just talking to my friends." The teacher doesn't want to hear what you've got to say. He just wants you to move to the end of the line. You don't want to hear what the teacher has to say. All you want to do is warn your friends that another group is sitting where you usually sit. It never even crosses your mind that there are other empty tables that you and your buddies can occupy, without a hassle. You don't yet realize that it's small stuff that you are allowing to cause you big problems.

The teacher says, "Go to the end of the line, or go to my office, and I don't want to hear any back talk from you." Now of course with all of your buddies standing right there and everyone else in the immediate vicinity listening, you can't just *go to the end of the line in silence.* So you decide to just warn your friends quickly and move on, but in order to do this, you must ignore the teacher's warning and talk to your friends. You tell yourself, *this won't take but a few seconds,* without realizing those few seconds will cost you dearly.

Results: you get a three-day suspension for insubordination. During this three-day period, you don't get to play in the basketball tournament that takes place the day following your suspension, and you get grounded by your parents for a two-week period. All of this because you didn't think, you merely reacted. You didn't allow yourself to realize what a small thing it would have been for you and your friends to sit at one of the unoccupied tables. You permitted yourself to sweat a small, unimportant thing and you caused yourself unnecessary stress and distress, not to mention the loss of fun that playing in and being at the game would have brought.

You can be a happy, well-adjusted young person if you make up your mind that you will not let the *small stuff* in your life drive you crazy. Whenever things happen that are unpleasant, and know that unpleasant things happen in everybody's life, make a genuine effort to keep them in perspective. Determine not to create unnecessary drama but to accept that *this too shall pass*, and get on with the business of living your pleasant life in spite of the infrequent occurrences of unpleasantness. Do not believe, as Chicken Little, that the sky is falling, whenever you are faced with one of life's difficulties or unpleasant situations. I hasten to assure you that it isn't!

2.

Mistakes Are Part of Life

Make peace with the reality that *mistakes are a natural part of life.* I do not mean to suggest that you intentionally do things that would usually be considered mistakes or unintentional occurrences. What I do mean to suggest is that you should be aware of the fact that things happen in life, in everybody's life, over which an individual has no control and which we all wish had not happened.

It is all right to wish that something that happens in your life had not happened. But let the wish be fleeting. Don't dwell on it; don't use up a great amount of your life energy wishing. Instead, focus on what you need to do to get past it without causing yourself additional stress and without making matters worse. Use your energy to correct the error if it is something that you can correct, and to figure out whether the mistake is your mistake and therefore, one that you need to correct.

Learn to discern when an error is yours to correct and when it is somebody else's to make right. Don't try to fix other people's mistakes. Don't try to be like the mythological *Atlas* and carry the weight of the whole world on your shoulders. To do so might give you a temporary *high* or feeling of power, but let me hasten to assure you that carrying other people's burdens can become mighty taxing.

Even when the mistake is yours, it might not be one you can fix. Accept this as one of life's learned lessons: *all of our mistakes are not correctable ones; some of them can be corrected; some are not correctable.* And when we make mistakes that we cannot correct, we must learn from them and get on with the business of living. Sweating over an error that you can do nothing about is counterproductive. In other words, it is hindering rather than serving the purpose of helping you to learn from the mistake so that hopefully, you won't repeat it, and then move on.

Learn to discern the difference between a mistake and disobedience. For example, if your mother says, "Please don't handle that vase. It isn't very expensive, but it has sentimental value because it's one of the few things that I have left of my mother's." But you decide to handle the vase anyhow, and then you drop the vase and break it. *That's not a mistake. That's disobedience!* You didn't accidentally handle the vase. You made a conscious decision to pick it up. Learn the difference and accept that there is a difference!

As you accept that mistakes are a natural part of life and that everybody makes them, you'll be able to move past a mistake without unduly sweating it and you will be a more contented person as a result. Accept that mistakes are a part of everyone's life. No one is perfect; everyone makes mistakes and that as a person, you're bound to make a few yourself! When you understand that this is so, you'll be well on your way creating a happier you.

3.

Determination Is Important

Have you ever noticed what happens when you make up your mind to do something? Take a few minutes and reflect on a time when you made up your mind that you were going to accomplish something. It doesn't matter what it was. It might have been to pass a certain test, or to go to a certain dance or party, or to get your parent's permission for some activity in which you were interested.

What is important about it is the *determination* to be successful propelled you to work hard and to do whatever was necessary to accomplish your goal.

Now think about how many times you were successful when you were determined. Chances are good that there have been very few, if any, failures you can recall when you really made up your mind to accomplish something. And I want you to know that this is true of almost everyone. When a person really makes up his or her mind to accomplish something, success is not far behind.

Determination is the act of making or arriving at a decision. The wonderful thing about determination is that it is always within your control. Unlike correcting a mistake or wishing an error away, you get to control the strength of your determination. If you make up your mind that you are going to do well in school, then you *will* do your homework, you *will* go to bed at a reasonable hour, you *will* be attentive in class, you will… well, you get the picture. Make the determination to succeed, and you *will*!

Do not sweat the little failures that you will encounter from time to time. Understand that success does not mean never failing. Success means never giving up. It means that quitting is not an option. When you really want to accomplish a worthy goal, *stick with it until it is done*. If you proceed with the understanding that quitting is not an option, your success is assured.

4.

Avoid Negative Thoughts

Do not allow yourself to be absorbed with negative thoughts. Don't dwell on negativity. There are many more positive things that happen in your life than there are negative things, but if you are not tuned in to this reality, you can find yourself thinking about the negative a lot more than you do the positive.

Say, for example, that you forgot you had a math test covering negative integers. You didn't review what you had learned in class as your teacher asked you to do. Then you arrive for math class, take your seat and read the following on the board: Take out a cover sheet. Quiz today covering negative integers.

You immediately think: *I forgot all about the quiz she said we were going to have today. But I did understand the explanations our teacher gave us, I should do okay.*

The teacher hands out copies of the quiz. It has 20 items. You look over the quiz and immediately realize that you have forgotten what you thought you had learned about adding, subtracting and multiplying negative integers. There are 15 items which require you to remember the rules for adding and subtracting negative integers; only 5 items require you to multiply negative integers. You think, *if I could remember the rules for adding and subtracting them, I could pass this test with a "C". But I can't remember any of the rules. If only I had reviewed…*

You're still sitting there with hardly anything on your paper when the teacher says, "There are five minutes left for the test." You've been lamenting your failure to review for the past twenty-five minutes. Instead of trying to recall the rules you need in order to do well on the test, you've been *mentally kicking yourself* for failing to review.

Dwelling on the negative is another counterproductive time user. It does no good, and most of the time it causes you to not think about what you need to do so that the behavior that produced the negative in your life does not get repeated. *Do not dwell on the negative.*

Determine to learn from behaviors that produce negatives in your life, *learn from them,* and then get on with the business of living!

5.

Learn How to Ignore

Ignoring someone who has said something to you or about you that you don't like, or that is embarrassing, is impossible. Right? *Wrong!!* You can do it, but it takes determination and a measure of *self-control*.

Imagine you are in class; everything is quiet. Everybody seems to be doing the classwork. You are a very good student.

You've just noticed that Michael, sitting next to you, is rolling spitballs. He has two or three in the palm of his hand. You glance at him, but you are not going to *rat him out*. He sees you observe the spitballs and immediately he thinks you're going to tell.

"Nerd!" he loudly hisses. Now instead of ignoring him, which would definitely have been in your best interest, you retaliate.

"You're not talking to me!" you hiss back loudly. The teacher hears you, but she didn't hear the student who started the verbal ping-pong.

"There should be no talking at this time, and you know that," the teacher says as she stares hard at you. You tell the teacher that Michael started it by calling you a nerd. Michael, of course, denies it. You tell the teacher that Michael is lying. "Isn't he, Kay?" You ask Kay, the girl sitting to your right. Kay says nothing but shrugs her shoulders to indicate that she does not know and doesn't want to get involved.

The teacher lets you know, in no uncertain terms, that she is not pleased with the disruption you're causing. You feel angry and wronged. You feel that you are being *fussed at* for something that was caused by someone else. You have not yet realized that had you ignored Michael and continued with your classwork, the teacher would not be having this discussion with you.

Learn to ignore some things. Some comments should not be dignified with a response. Some comments have no dignity unless you lend dignity to them. Don't sweat them! Understand early in your life that you do not automatically become what someone calls you. Accept that it is complimentary to be intelligent and that other intelligent people know that this is so. Cultivate the idea that what you think of yourself is much more important than what some kid with less intelligence than you calls you.

If you are able to think of negative comments and foolish gibes as you would a gnat or a fly, quite annoying but definitely not worth your time and attention, then you will be able to avoid many potentially problematic situations in your life that can rob you of being the happy person that you deserve to be.

6.

Bullying

According to http://www.stopbullying.gov, bullying includes actions such as making threats, spreading rumors, attacking someone physically or verbally, and excluding someone from a group on purpose. This behavior is often repeated. It is usually lead by someone (or more than one) who is in some way more powerful than the other person. The stronger person may not always be physically stronger, but is somehow able to manipulate the weaker person. A bully may have been a victim of bullying at some point and in this way bullies are simply trying to get back for the treatment they were given.

Sometimes bullies engage in this behavior to impress others.

Bullying has always been a problem in schools. It didn't just start with your current generation. It can take various forms and affect all age levels, but you should know that it is wrong to bully someone and it is wrong to know that someone else is being bullied and fail to act.

Now you may be asking, "What do you mean by fail to act? What can I do?" Fail to act means that you do nothing. What can you do? You can tell someone in authority about the bullying. You can refuse to be part of the audience who observes the bullying with glee. You can decline to laugh or taunt and behave as if watching someone being bullied is sport.

In fact, in addition to acting upon what you have learned, you should not believe what bullies say about you. Don't sweat it if bullies say hateful things about you. Realize that bullies don't make smart decisions. If they did, they wouldn't be bullies. Ignore them unless they are threatening to harm you or someone else physically. In this case, it is extremely important to report this bullying behavior to a teacher, school counselor, or principal right away. Also, make your parents aware that this is happening.

Cyberbullying is also a major problem for school age kids and it is just as wrong as traditional bullying. It is similar to regular bullying in its intent and the target. It may be defined as willful and repeated harm inflicted through the use of electronic devices, such as computers, cellphones, and tablets. Examples of cyberbullying include mean text messages or emails, rumors sent by email or posted on social networking sites, and embarrassing pictures, videos, websites, or fake profiles, according to http://www.stopbullying.gov.

So you see, there are things that you can do to discourage bullying. Don't sweat it if you have peers who bully or who make sport of those being bullied. Accept that it is wrong, refuse to participate in it, and have the courage to report it!

7.

Let What You Think Be More Important to You

Do not think that because your friends or peers think a certain thing to be true about you, that it is automatically true. Say, for example, that you are a person with very dark skin. Some of your peers might think dark skin is unattractive. Or say, for example that you are a person with very fair skin and freckles. Some of your peers might express the opinion that fair skin and freckles are unattractive.

Never allow someone else's opinion to determine your opinion of yourself. Keep in mind that everyone has an opinion and that beauty is in the eyes of the looker. If you remember this, at times when some-expresses an opinion that is contrary to yours, or expresses an opinion that is unfavorable about you, you'll be able to keep it in proper perspective.

One of the main reasons why it is so important for you to get to know yourself is because when a person knows him or herself really well, that person is a lot less likely to take to heart other people's opinions. For example, if someone calls you stupid, but you know yourself to be an intelligent young person, you won't sweat it; you will find that it is not at all difficult to ignore the negative comment about yourself.

On the other hand, a very young child, perhaps of five or six years old, is more likely to believe him or herself to be stupid if he or she is called stupid. This is so because a child of five or six does not yet know him or herself well. Young children, therefore, take their opinions of themselves from the opinions they hear others express. One clear sign of maturity is being able to ignore negative comments other people make about you. Know yourself!

If you regularly interact with younger siblings or young children, it is very important that you reread and remember the preceding paragraph. Your influence on them is no small thing. You have the power to help these children decide how they will feel about themselves. Don't take it lightly. Your influence can have far-reaching ramifications.

Knowing yourself is very important. Knowing that you will influence your younger siblings as they begin the process of getting to know themselves is also powerful information that should be given serious consideration.

8.

Cultivate Positive Friends

As a young person, you are probably already aware of how important your friends are to you and of how much you respect the opinions of your friends. For these reasons, it is very important to cultivate positive friendships.

Maybe you are wondering what it means to cultivate positive friendships. It means that you make an effort to form relationships with other people who want to accomplish some worthwhile goals in their lives. It means that you seek relationships with other boys and girls who enjoy wholesome leisure time activities. It means that you choose your best friends from among the people who are *about something*. If you choose your best friends from among those boys and girls who are *about something*, then these will be positive people. You see, boys and girls who are *about something* make an effort to be successful. These are the boys and girls who do their homework. These are the boys and girls who cooperate with their parents and with their teachers. These are the boys and girls who get along well with their peers. These are the boys and girls who will respect your opinions and allow that you are entitled to them, even when their opinions differ from yours.

Positive peers will help you to make

decisions that are in *your* best interest. You can share some of your innermost thoughts and feelings with positive friends and know that they will not put a *negative spin* on your private expressions.

Begin early in your life to surround yourself with positive people. Become aware and alert to those boys and girls in your environment who are always making negative remarks about others. Know that when you are not in their presence, they are equally likely to make disparaging remarks about you. Negative people have formed the habit of negativity. Don't sweat it. Know that the world is made up of both negative and positive people, and you get to choose the people with whom you surround yourself.

Learn not to sweat negative remarks made by negative people. Realize that you do not have to cultivate relationships with negative people. Remember that you do not have to sweat these people or their remarks because you do not have to surround yourself with people who make you have negative and unhappy feelings.

You will be a happier person if you understand that negativity breeds negativity and the converse is also true. If you surround yourself with people who think in a positive way and are encouraging, you are likely to take on positive attributes as you are filled with positive feelings that breed success.

9.

You Can Be a Winner

Remember our earlier discussion about determination? Well, determination is the main ingredient in the *winner's recipe*. It is the first step on the journey to success. Whatever your goal, whether short-term or long-term, in order to achieve it, you must first determine to do so.

Determination is the easy part. It involves a mindset. Next comes the not so easy part: *the work*. The work that you'll have to do in order to achieve your goal depends upon the goal that you want to accomplish. Let's say, for example, that a certain young person named Michael has made the decision that he wants to go to college when he graduates from high school. He is now a freshman in high school. As the son of a single parent, he already knows that his mother will not be able to pay college tuition and other expenses associated with college for him.

He's had numerous discussions with his counselor, so he knows that all of the kids who maintain a 3.5 or better grade point average during each of their years in high school will be offered scholarships to college. Michael is determined to be one of those students. He was an excellent student throughout elementary and middle school, so he has the foundation in place that will allow him to maintain the needed grade point average.

Michael does very well during his freshman year. In fact, his grade point average at the end of the year is 3.8. He is pleased that so far he has stayed on track and has achieved the goal that he set for himself as a freshman.

The sophomore year for Michael begins with great expectations. His counselor and teachers know of his excellent academic record and have high expectations for him. He has high expectations for himself, and the confidence that success breeds. Riding this high, he meets Luby, a junior who isn't sure if she's going to graduate with her class but takes the attitude, *so what? It'll happen if it happens!*

Luby is a very attractive girl and Michael is flattered that a junior *has eyes for him.* The two of them begin to date. At first they only date on weekends. They go to a matinee because it's early and Michael still has time after the date to review and do whatever else is necessary to keep his grades up. He has shared his plans with Luby and she agrees that they are fine plans. At first she is encouraging, but as time passes, Luby wants to go dancing after the matinee. Later she takes to calling Michael during the week interrupting his studies just to hear his voice.

Michael talks with her for a while and then he tells her gently, but firmly that he needs to get back to his homework. After all, Michael's classes are all college prep and his calculus class is tough. They say good-bye, but fifteen minutes later, the phone rings again. Again it is Luby.

"What you doing?" she asks. His first thought is, *the same thing I was doing when you called fifteen minutes ago: studying*. But Michael doesn't want to lose Luby. He really does like her, and they have fun together, more fun than he's ever had with a girl before. Luby's adventuresome and daring, and she's an exciting girl. If he says this to her, what will she think of him? Will she think he's immature and too young for her? Will she tell the other kids that he's a nerd? At this point, Michael has begun to sweat *small stuff* that can derail his plans for college. He needs to renew his determination. He needs to take the time to refocus. My advice to the Michaels of the world is simple: your plans for your future are more important than maintaining a relationship with someone who is not supportive of the goals you have for yourself. They are more important than what someone who is not supportive of your goals will say about you to others. Don't sweat it. Stay on track. Remember that success is not a destination. It is a journey!

10.

Winners Never Quit

Michael is now a senior and has maintained the required 3.5 or better grade point average throughout his freshman, sophomore and junior years of high school. His senior year has just begun and he is definitely expecting to be one of the seniors to receive a scholarship offer.

Shortly after school begins, Michael makes an appointment with his counselor. During the session, she tells him that scholarship offerings are down this year. "With your fine academic record, you definitely qualify for a scholarship offer, but with the cutback, it's going to be more competitive this year," she tells him.

Michael begins to worry: maybe I've done all of that studying for nothing. Maybe I won't even get a scholarship after all.

Michael broke up with his girlfriend toward the end of his freshmen year and hasn't had a serious girlfriend since then. He is serious about his grades, but most of his buddies aren't interested in that sort of thing. Most of them will feel lucky if they can manage to pass the exit exam and graduate from high school, period.

Michael passed the exit exam on his first try as a sophomore in high school, which is the level at which it is given to high school students initially, so that isn't his concern. But he is concerned about getting that scholarship for which he has worked for years in order to qualify, and now he's even more nervous about it. He decided to make an appointment with his counselor and have a heart-to-heart talk.

As soon as he arrives and is greeted by the counselor he blurts, "What are my chances of getting a scholarship?"

The counselor does not want to mislead Michael. She tells him truthfully that he has as good a chance as every other student who qualifies, but that this year the school has more qualifying students than scholarship offers. She says that this is first year that this has happened since she has been at the school. "I don't know what I'm gonna do if I don't get a scholarship," Michael says, almost as if he is thinking aloud.

"Think about this alternative," the counselor tells Michael. "The army has a program that allows a person who enlists to earn and save money for college. The army provides matching funds. You can save more than thirty thousand dollars during a two-year period of military service."

"What does a person have to do to earn this money?" Michael asks. The counselor explains to Michael that there will be army recruiters coming to the school and that there will be an assembly for interested juniors and seniors.

"The recruiters will be able to explain the particulars a lot more clearly than I can," she tells him. "The assembly is being planned for Tuesday of next week," she concludes.

Michael is breathing a little easier as he leaves the counselor's office and heads for his advanced English class. He is just starting to learn an important lesson: It is not a good practice to put all of your eggs in one basket. In other words, always have an alternative plan.

In life, things do not always work out the way we want them to or the way we have planned. When a plan does not work out, sweating it does not change anything, so don't sweat it, kid. It's not the time to give up. Winners do not quit.

11.

Attitude Is Everything (Almost)

It has been said, and truthfully so, that one's attitude determines one's altitude. What this means is how high or how far one goes in life or how much a person is able to accomplish, is determined, to a very large degree, by one's attitude. A person's attitude is his or her *state of mind* or *feeling*. This being the case, the attitude that you internalize and display in any given situation, is very important.

Let's consider the following example.

Two girls, Tamala and Pamela are twin sisters. Their parents dropped them off at the mall Saturday morning at eleven o'clock. They had permission to do some shopping, have lunch, and then to go to a two o'clock matinee to see a popular teen movie.

The girls had lunch and did their shopping, as planned. They rented a small locker in the mall to store their purchases. They then walked to the multiplex theater in the mall to purchase their tickets for the movie.

As they are approaching the ticket office, they can see the titles of numerous movies currently showing. Several of them are adult movies. Tamala notices that a popular adult movie is showing at a two o'clock matinee.

"Let's go see that movie instead," she said pointing at the poster advertising an adult movie. I've wanted to see that movie ever since it came out. A couple of kids at school who saw it said it was really good."

Pamela agrees. They purchase the tickets and go to see the movie. Each agrees that it was an exciting movie and they had enjoyed watching it. As they are leaving the movie theater, they are discussing the movie and almost bump into Mrs. Gonzales, their next door neighbor and one of their mother's closest friends. Fleetingly, Mrs. Gonzales wonders if their mother gave the twins permission to watch that movie, but she doesn't articulate any of this to the girls as they say hello to one another and move on.

Several days later, Mrs. Gonzales and the twins' mother encounter one another at the grocery store. Both have stopped to get loaves of bread. They chat briefly and then Mrs. Gonzales mentions that she bumped into the twins as they were leaving the theater in the mall a few days ago. She told their mother about the movie she went to see and mentioned that the twins saw it too. "It was a bit strong for fourteen-year old girls," she remarks.

Later that evening when Tamala arrives home from school her mother says, "Tamala, I know that you went to see a movie that you knew I wouldn't have given you permission to see."

Tamala immediately assumes a defensive attitude. "That old biddy, Gonzales needs to get a life and mind her own business," she says heatedly.

Her mother tells her, "Mrs. Gonzales was minding her business. Like it or not, all children are all adults' business.

And I don't like your attitude about this not one bit! Go to your room. You're on phone and television restriction for the next two weeks. And don't even think about that dance Saturday night!"

When Pamela arrives home from her piano lesson, her mother confronts her just as she has Tamala. Unlike her twin sister, Pamela assumes an apologetic attitude. "I'm so sorry, Mom. We really didn't lie to you. We had meant to see the movie you gave us permission to see, but we changed our minds when we realized that there was a matinee performance of the other movie."

Because of Pamela's apologetic attitude, she did not get put on punishment. She was admonished by her mother not to do it again. Her mother told her, "If I have not agreed that you and your sister can see a particular movie, then you can take for granted that you do not have permission to see it, and this is especially true if the movie is not rated for teen audiences."

Becoming defensive when you have done something wrong does not help your case. If you are wrong, don't try to lay the blame on someone else. Learning to assume responsibility for your own errors is something that everyone needs to do. Don't sweat it. Accept it as a natural part of becoming a responsible human being.

12.

It's Your Decision

There are some decisions that no one can make but you. If you have good, effective parents in your life, you are indeed fortunate because they can help guide you in your decisions.

But not every child has that, and none of us are in a position to choose our parents. The parents and other relatives that you get are not yours by choosing. Your connection to them are the results of choices made long before you are born.

But some decisions in life are your decisions. *You* get to choose, and the choices that you make will determine, to a great extent, your success or failure in life. Furthermore, some decisions that you have to make are ones that you and you alone can make. Nobody else can make them for you, not even good, effective parents.

Say that you are given an assignment in your reading class to read a certain book, and the teacher says that you have three weeks to read the book. She tells the class that there will be a test covering the book and that the test will count for a double grade.

You already know what the title of the book is and how many pages are in the book. You mentally calculate that since there are 21 days in a three-week period and the book has 274 pages, you'll need to read at least thirteen pages each day.

The day that the assignment is given, you meant to ask your mother to stop by a bookstore to get the book for you on the way home from school, but you forgot. In bed that night you suddenly remember that you didn't mention the book to your mom because you forgot about it, and now you can't get the head start you'd decided to get by reading ten or so pages before falling asleep. *That's okay*, you tell yourself, *I'll definitely get started tomorrow.*

The next day comes. You don't have the class requiring the book, so you don't think about the book again until heading for the class the following day and you see several of your classmates with the book as they enter the classroom. *Oh gosh! I've got to remember to get that book*, you say to yourself. Not only did you fail to get the head start you had intended, but you're already behind the schedule you set for yourself as well.

As soon as you get into the car, you think about asking your mother to stop by a bookstore, but you know her well enough to know that you'll have to explain it *all* to her. *And then she'll cram the whole book down my throat*, you tell yourself. *She won't let me do it by my own schedule.* So instead you say, "Mom, you don't have to pick me up tomorrow. Sandra's mom is picking her up and she says I can get a ride home with them."

You're already thinking about how you can get to the mall's bookstore and buy the book before going home tomorrow. It hasn't even crossed your mind that by tomorrow you'll be even farther behind.

Finally, you get the book. You had intended to sit at one of the tables in the food court at the mall and get started reading it, but as soon as you arrive at the food court, there are several of your friends at a table. They invite you to join them, and of course, you do. Thoughts of the book, and getting started on it, are the furthest things from your mind at the moment.

Eventually you do manage to get started on the book, but by now you are so far behind that it's going to be hard to catch up. You mentally revise the initial schedule you'd set. *Instead of thirteen pages daily, you'll read at least twenty pages*, you tell yourself. And you really mean to do it, but the book is boring and it's hard to stick with it for twenty, whole pages. Before you realize it, the three weeks have elapsed and you are sitting in the class staring at a major test, and are clueless about most of the questions.

At this point, I believe you get the picture. Even if the student had been honest with her mother and explained *it all*, that's no guarantee that she would have done the required reading. You see, reading a book is one clear example of a choice that no one can make for you but you.

To make the choice to read a book, you've got to be willing to not sweat stuff like giving up some social time with your friends, or missing a favorite television program. Remember, the choices you make will determine, to a great extent, your failure or success, and not just of a single project, but in life.

13.

Nobody Gets to Choose

There are some choices in life that you do not get to make. You have absolutely no control over who your father is or who your mother is or who your relatives are; neither does anybody else. Most people, if they could choose, would choose *exactly who they've got* because these are the people most of us know and love. But even if you *would* choose differently, don't sweat it. It will be wasted sweat since you don't get the choice. But what you do get to choose are how you act and react in given circumstances and situations as you interact with people, relatives and others.

You don't get to choose who your classmates are, or who is seated on either side of you in each of your classes. Since this is so, don't sweat it. If your worst enemy is seated right next to you in one of your classes, you don't have the option of changing his or her seat, or your own. But you do get to choose how you

behave. You can take your seat, say hello courteously and do your work, or you can sit there and give him or her the evil eye, make snide remarks and… Well, you get the picture. There are some choices that are not yours to make, and using an excuse like, *it wouldn't have happened if such and such a person had not been sitting next to me, or if I had better parents, or if he hadn't said that or if she hadn't done that,* does no good.

What someone else does or does not do is something you cannot choose. But you are in control of what you do and of what you do not do. This being the case, don't sweat a choice that is not yours to make. Make good choices that are in your best interest when the choice is yours to make, and you will have a head start on the road to success. Don't use any of your life energy to sweat a choice that is not one you can make. Nothing will be gained and there are many potential losses.

14.

Opportunity Never Outstays Her Welcome

There are some choices in life that you do not get to make. You have absolutely no control over who your father is or who your mother is or who your relatives are; neither does anybody else. Most people, if they could choose, would choose *exactly who they've got* because these are the people most of us know and love. But even if you *would* choose differently, don't sweat it. It will be wasted sweat since you don't get the choice. But what you do get to choose are how you act and react in given circumstances and situations as you interact with people, relatives and others.

You don't get to choose who your classmates are, or who is seated on either side of you in each of your classes. Since this is so, don't sweat it. If your worst enemy is seated right next to you in one of your classes, you don't have the option of changing his or her seat, or your own. But you do get to choose how you behave. You can take your seat, say hello courteously and do your work, or you can sit there and give him or her the evil eye, make snide remarks and… Well, you get the picture. There are some choices that are not yours to make, and using an excuse like, *it wouldn't have happened if such and such a person had not been sitting next to me, or if I had better parents, or if he hadn't said that or if she hadn't done that,* does no good.

What someone else does or does not do is something you cannot choose. But you are in control of what you do and of what you do not do. This being the case, don't sweat a choice that is not yours to make. Make good choices that are in your best interest when the choice is yours to make, and you will have a head start on the road to success. Don't use any of your life energy to sweat a choice that is not one you can make. Nothing will be gained and there are many potential losses.

15.

Where There's a Will...

I know you've heard the axiom, *where there's a will, there's a way*. And it's been proven repeatedly that it is a true saying.

The word *will* refers to the mental faculty by which one deliberately chooses or decides on a course of action. It alludes to the determination discussed earlier. There is nothing stronger than *the will*. I have known deaf people who learned to dance in spite of the fact that they could not hear the beat of the music, because they had the *will* to dance. I have known a regular man who was able to amass superhuman strength to lift an automobile that was crushing his beloved child, because of the *will* to do so.

How strong is *your will* to succeed? Do you even know? Have you thought about what it will take in order for you to graduate from high school, get accepted into college or other job training type of program, and become a contributing member of society? If you have not thought about it, it's not too late, and certainly not too early to give it some serious thought. Graduating from high school or college or completing on-the-job training, or enlisting in a branch of military service, to name a few examples, are not things that just happen to those of us who keep on living. Some planning, and some intellectual directives are involved. In other words, people who become productive members of society must make use of their mental faculties to deliberately choose their course of action.

If you have not done so up to this point, don't sweat it, but don't continue to put off giving some serious thought to the course you want your life to take. Even though you probably will change your mind several times before you make a final decision about your course, now is the time to begin thinking about what you want to do with your life.

When you decide early in life what it is you'd like to become, then you begin to see the relevance of pursuing a certain course of action. This brings a certain structure and focus to your existence, and it doesn't matter if you change your mind more than once.

What matters is that you begin to practice being focused. It's important that you begin to understand early in your life that whatever anybody practices the most is what he or she learns to do best.

Determine that you will practice becoming a focused young person. Focus brings clarity to why it is that you are pursuing a certain course of action. It can yield dividends that can help to make you a well-adjusted, more *in control of your destiny*, individual.

16.

Somebody Will Help

As a young person, it is very important for you to know that no matter what you're going through, and no matter how hard things seem to be at any given moment in time, there is always help available. When an individual is aware that this is so, he or she is much less likely to become discouraged when the going gets rough. And you might as well know that the going gets rough for most people at one time or another in their lives.

Learn early in your life that the problems and difficulties you encounter as you make your way from childhood and adolescence to adulthood do not have to be viewed as if the sky is falling. Take a step back to gain perspective. Become a thinking young person. Learn to self-counsel. Ask yourself questions like, *what could I have done differently to have avoided this situation? Could I have avoided this situation? Is this a problem that I can fix? What do I need to do now? Do I need to talk with someone about this?*

Remember our earlier discussions and recognize that you cannot fix every problem that you must deal with. Learn to control those things in your life over which you have some control. For example, there are some lines you shouldn't even go near, let alone cross. *Keep clear of these lines.* If you know, for example, that some of your peers are heading for trouble because you're privy to their plans to say, start a fight after school or cut school, then you are obligated to yourself to steer clear of them and even to tell someone in authority. Keep in mind that you are equally guilty if you allow people to hurt others or themselves simply because you do not want to tell on them.

Don't sweat it if someone calls you a tattletale. That's small stuff. But someone being hurt, kids being jailed, parents paying fines, which is what some school systems have begun to do when kids cut school, none of these things can be thought of as small stuff.

There are always people who are willing to help you, but you must be willing to ask for help. You must be willing to let someone know that you need help. Never lose sight of that. There are *always* adults who are willing to listen to you, and it's very important for you to remember that this is so. And you also need to remember that no matter how complicated the situation seems, there is help available.

You do not have to handle your problems alone. There are no insurmountable problems, just problems that seem insurmountable at the moment that you are faced with them. Don't try to *go it alone*. You don't have to. You have a choice.

17.

Social Media

Life as a teenager can be complicated enough. Add social media/social networking into the mix and you add a whole other layer of complexity to the already complex social interactions of you and your peers. There has been much speculation on the kinds of effects technology has on young people in your age group.

Do you have social media/social networking accounts? If you do, that's fine, just make sure that you use them as they are supposed to be used and that you don't allow them to distract you or to cause you to make bad decisions. There are many good things you can do with your social media accounts, and there are also some bad things. It depends on how you use them.

Learn early in your life that most of the things in which you become involved will present you with possible advantages as well as disadvantages, and Facebook and other social media sites are no exceptions.

If you consider the multimedia experience you are surrounded with (cell phones, computers, tablets, portable gaming systems, etc.), it makes sense that frequently checking and posting on your social media accounts cause interruptions and distractions. This is certainly a disadvantage when you consider that middle school, high school and college students who check Facebook or other social media at least once during a 15-minute study period achieved lower grades.

Do not sweat your peers' opinions, especially if they are pressuring you to get social media accounts. Do so if you want and if your parents agree with the idea, but be aware that there is no rush to do so and that you're not missing out on any necessities if you don't.

Using social media can promote good social skills because it allows you to keep up with current friends and make new ones. You can share photos with friends, but never upload inappropriate photos. It's also important to remember not to reveal personal information about yourself and don't accept strangers as "friends".

Remember, cyberbullying is willful and repeated harm inflicted through the use of electronic devices, such as computers, cellphones, and tablets. Examples of cyberbullying include mean text messages or emails, rumors sent by email or posted on social networking sites, and embarrassing pictures, videos, websites, or fake profiles, according to http://www.stopbullying.gov. Be a courageous young person who is willing to report this if it happens to you or someone you know.

Do not spend too much time on social media sites. Your time is valuable, impossible to retrieve, and should be used wisely. Don't sweat it if you have friends who spend too much time on these sites. You are responsible for doing what you know is right for you!

So you can see that social media sites have advantages and disadvantages, and it's up to you and your parents to decide if using them is right for you.

18.

Don't Cop Out

If you decide to join the band at school, and your parents buy you a trumpet, don't cop out if you don't like practicing anymore after a month or two. A month or two are not long enough for you to make that decision intelligently. Don't sweat it if, at that point, you don't like the practice. Stick with it for at least one full school term, then you might feel quite differently. Chances are good that you will enjoy learning to play the trumpet and chances are equally good that you will meet other people who are in the band with whom you enjoy interacting. But even if you find that you really do not like it and really do not want to persevere, after a full school year, you will be in a position to make an intelligent decision about whether or not you want to give it up.

You should know that one of the things that label people as intelligent is how they make decisions about the things that affect their lives. But in order for anybody to make an intelligent decision, some thought must go into it. Take the time to give careful thought before you make a decision that can impact your life.

There are many kids who thought they didn't like playing an instrument or taking a certain class or playing a certain sport or riding a bike or…(you get the picture), only to learn that they really do like the activity, but they had prematurely made the decision to cop out. The only reason they didn't quit is because their parents did not allow them to do so at the point at which they wanted to quit. Their parents were wise and experienced enough to recognize that they had not been involved in the activity long enough to make an intelligent decision about liking or disliking it. You see, anybody can say, *I'm frustrated; I'm quitting*. But it takes a special person, an intelligent, thinking person to say, "I'm not enjoying this, but I haven't stuck with it long enough to know whether or not I will learn to like it." Give yourself *that* chance whenever you think about *copping out* of any worthy endeavor. When you have honestly given it adequate time to make an intelligent decision, if you really do not like it and do not wish to continue with it, chances are good that your parents will be supportive of your decision.

19.

Know the Rules

It is very important that you know the rules whenever there are rules by which you must be governed. As the saying goes, *ignorance of the law is no excuse*. How many times have you heard someone use as an excuse, *I didn't know?* And while we can all accept that a small child, say one of three or four years old, really *did not know*, most of us tend to be suspicious of others who break a rule and use as their excuse, *I didn't know.*

One of the main reasons why *I didn't know* is not a valid excuse is because you are responsible for *knowing* before *doing*. Say that your sister goes into your room to borrow your lip gloss. The next morning you reach into the place where you usually keep it only to discover that it isn't there. You immediately suspect that she has borrowed it, so you ask her if she has seen your lip gloss. She admits to having it in her purse. She tells you that she meant to put it back, but forgot. You tell her she should've asked before taking it, but she says she didn't think you'd mind. "If you had asked me, you could've found out whether or not I would have minded," you tell her. In other words, she was responsible for *knowing* before *doing*. And guess what? So is everybody else.

Before you do something that could be potentially damaging or hurtful to yourself or to somebody else, take the time to think before you act. Ask yourself, *do I know what the rules are? Am I sure this is something that I should do? Do I want to get involved in this?*

When you take the time to know what the rules are, you will not end up having to sweat the consequences that can result when you act without knowledge of the rules.

20.

Follow the Rules

You need to learn early in your life that rules exist for a very important reason. Without rules there is anarchy and chaos. But knowing the rules will not be of benefit to you if you do not follow the rules.

Let's say that John knows that the rule in his home is lights out and in bed no later than 11 on school nights. But on this particular night, their dad is out-of-town on a business trip and their mother left them home alone to do some Christmas shopping. Because she is buying gifts for them and doesn't want them to see what she's buying, she tells them to finish with their homework and get ready for bed, that she'll be home soon.

John is a junior in high school and his brother is in eighth grade, so their mother feels that they are quite capable of staying home alone for a few hours. Because they are not sure where she went, they have no way of gauging when she'll return.

John and his brother, Adam, completed their homework more than an hour ago. They've played a couple of video games and had their showers. Now John turns on the television and channel surfs for a few seconds. An old John Wayne movie is coming on. John loves the old westerns and he and Adam settle down in front of the television on an old quilt with sofa pillows. The movie came on at ten o'clock and will end around midnight.

At 11:15 Adam says he's sleepy and is going to bed. John tells him he wants to see how the movie will end, so Adam goes to bed, but John stays up. He doesn't see the end of the movie, however, because he falls asleep before the movie ends.

Of course their mother arrives home and observes him asleep on the quilt instead of in his bed. Results: John is put on punishment for two weeks; no television, no video games, and one of the items his mother bought for him is withheld. He doesn't get it for Christmas as she had intended, and as he had requested. She gives it to him three months later for his birthday in March.

Don't sweat it because your home has rules and it seems that none of your friends or peers have to put up with the stuff that you do. Chances are good that most of them, if not all of them, have rules in their homes too. And you can bet that the ones who don't are living in chaos. Remember that rules exist for a reason, and when you follow the rules, you are usually better off for having done so.

21.

Don't Argue

When you argue with your parents or other people in authority, you are setting yourself up for unhappiness, displeasure and failure. You *can't win*. Recognize this as a fact of your life, and you will save yourself a lot of sweat, anxiety and frustration.

Recall all the times when you allowed yourself to get into an argument with one or both of your parents and you were the loser. Now try to think of the times when this happened and you were the winner. Chances are very good that you lost considerably more times than you won, if you ever won. And even the few times when you managed to wear them down and get your own way, you still did not win because you generated family discord and when this happens, no one in the family wins. Happy families are winning families and winning families are happy families!

Accept that your parents know what is best for you, that they love you, and that they are looking out for your best interest. Accept and respect the fact that your parents are responsible for you and that as good parents, they take this responsibility seriously. Once you accept this, try to keep it in focus. If you do, you will find yourself thinking before you respond in a way that provokes an argument. You will also begin to accept that you have an obligation to them just as they have to you. And while your obligation to your parents is not the same as theirs to you, you are just as responsible for meeting your obligation to them as they are for meeting theirs to you.

Most teens have no problem understanding and articulating that their parents *owe them*, and they do. But teens also need to accept and understand that *the obligation is not all one-sided.* Parents should love, nurture and take care of their children. Children should love, respect and obey their parents. When parents and children meet their obligations to one another, families live harmoniously. And who doesn't want a harmonious family life? But when you pout and argue because you can't get your way, you create disharmony in the family. Is this what you want to do?

ably not. Then don't do it.

Make and honor a silent pledge that you will not argue with your parents and that you will accept *No* from them without the usual bickering and pouting that creates disharmony in the family. Resolve to live unselfishly and to think about how you make your parents feel when their beloved child intentionally shows disrespect by arguing with their decisions.

If you have younger siblings, think of the example you are setting for them. Bear in mind that the decisions your parents make are in your best interest. Don't sweat the *No's*. Accept that your parents know best, and honor that. Soon enough you will be on your own and able to make your own decisions.

22.

Did You Really Mean That?

"I hate you!" You yell in a heated argument with your mother. Of course she's pretty upset at this point too and she says that *the feeling is mutual*. Hours later you are in your room still thinking about the heated words. And though you were very angry when you yelled those hateful words, you didn't really mean them. You felt that you meant them at the moment they were said, yet you knew even then, in your heart, that you did not and do not hate your mother. And although you know you shouldn't have said those words, your heart aches because your mother said that *the feeling is mutual*.

You've given no thought to your mother's feelings of hurt, but you've given lots of thought to your own feelings. You tell yourself that *parents should not tell their children they hate them. That was mean of mom to say that to me.* You have not allowed yourself to admit that the hateful words were yours. *The feeling is mutual*, are not hateful words. Had you said, "I love you," the refrain, *The feeling is mutual*, would have had a completely different connotation.

Are you beginning to see the importance of not arguing with your parents? Is the picture emerging a little more clearly?

When you don't argue with your parents, these kinds of hurtful situations and damaged feelings can usually be avoided. Words are not like pieces of candy or a book that you can retrieve. Once words are spoken, they can never be taken back. They become a part of your eternity. If you don't really mean it, *then don't say it.*

Learn to *swallow some thoughts* before they become words. You know you love your parents and you know they love you. Let the love you feel for them and the love they have for you motivate you to stop yourself from saying hurtful things. You'll be a happier person and you'll contribute to a more pleasant family life for yourself and for your family if you make the effort to swallow some thoughts and do not allow them to become words.

Any teenager can argue and pout and be surly, but it takes a special teen, one who can unselfishly put aside his or her own feelings and think about the feelings of the other family members, in order to be willing to swallow some thoughts before they can become words that disrupt the smooth flow of family life. Are you that special teen?

23.

Cultivate Your Compassion

When someone makes a joke at school at another child's expense, do you join in the laughter? Do you ever think about how you would feel if you were that kid? Did you ever think: *that's not very nice or that was unkind?*

Cultivate the capacity to put yourself mentally into someone else's place. Take a few minutes to think about how the person probably feels and how you would feel in the same or a similar situation. In other words, begin to cultivate your compassion. Sometimes when you are having a quiet moment alone, think about something unkind you may have said to your mom or dad. Now visualize yourself as the parent of a child you love dearly. Try to imagine how you would feel if this child who you love with all your heart said these very same words to you in the same or a very similar situation. If you will do this from time to time, you can begin to develop your compassion.

Compassion is defined as sympathetic concern for the suffering of another, together with the desire to help. Compassionate people are kind and are usually well-liked. Com- passionate people are sensitive to the feelings of others.

Don't sweat it because there will be some people who will mistake your kindness for weakness. Recognize that *kindness is not a weakness, rather it is a strength.* Anyone can laugh at someone else's expense, but it takes a strong person to stand up and refuse to do so. Anyone can bully a smaller child, but it takes strength to speak up on the child's behalf. Develop your compassion and you will be a better, happier person.

24.

Listen Carefully

Cultivate the ability to listen carefully whether you are in class and your teacher is talking, or you are having a heart to heart with your parents, or you are having a conversation with a friend. A good listener is an asset in any situation. And not just an asset to others, but an asset to him or herself.

Good listeners are rare. Notice how

frustrating it is when you are having a conversation with someone and you can hardly get a word in. Obviously the person is not a good listener. Equally obvious is the fact that the person is not interested in what you have to say. This kind of behavior also gives the impression that the person does not consider whatever you have to say of value.

Good listeners are able to avoid giving the impression that what another has to say is of no value. Being able to listen without interrupting the other person is a valuable skill to possess. It fosters good relationships. It makes the other person feel important. It gives the impression that you value the other person as well as what the other person has to say.

Don't sweat it if others interrupt you. Don't allow the rude behavior of others to be the example you choose to follow.

There will always be people who are not good listeners, but you do not have to be one of them. This is a choice that *you* get to make. Don't sweat it if you are not already a good listener. You can become one. It takes conscious effort and time, but it yields huge dividends.

25.

Seek Peace

If you seek peace, if peace is really what you want in your environment, then you can have it. But you must be willing to contribute to this peace. If, for example, your mom is always on your back about your messy room. The solution to this is simple: keep your room less messy. Now I know it's easier said than done, but you will be surprised how much easier it becomes when it's really what *you* want to do. A change in behavior is usually not easy, but a change is possible.

Most people desire peace in their environments, but many of the people who will say that they desire peace do not contribute to peace in their environments. Take, for example, the person who has allowed him or herself to acquire bad driving habits. It's not that this person is unaware of the laws governing drivers. It isn't that this person doesn't realize that poor driving habits increase the risks of accidents. It's just that this person does not consciously focus on the realization that his or her behavior is doing the opposite of contributing to peace in his or her environment.

Consider how Jan's behavior contributes to the lack of peace in her environment. Jan says that she is peace-loving and wants to live a peaceful existence. She has just completed all of her high school requirements. She could begin taking classes at the local community college but her parents have given her the option of taking classes or working. In fact, her parents had a heart to heart talk with her shortly before she completed semester exams. They told her that they would not allow her to do nothing for an entire semester. She agreed that she had no desire to do nothing, that she wanted to work instead of enroll at the community college.

Jan made the decision to work during the final semester of the school term. Now the school term has been in progress for five weeks and Jan is *still not working*. She sleeps until noon on most days, and then she is up until 2-3 a.m. every morning. Of course she isn't sleepy like the other members of her family. She has slept until noon.

Jan's parents are getting increasingly upset with her. They have tried talking with her about this behavior, but to no avail. Jan says she can't find a job, but it's clear to her parents that she is not exerting very much effort toward looking for one. How could she be doing so if she's sleeping until noon? And besides, Jan is enjoying sleeping until noon and staying up until the wee hours of the morning. But of course she doesn't share this with her parents. Jan is not contributing to peace in her environment.

26.

Is It Really That Bad?

Having to obey your parents can be annoying at times, but is it really that bad? Think about it. There are many boys and girls who do not have parents to love and guide them, and chances are good that they would trade places with you in a heartbeat if they could. Think of allegiance and obedience as equitable trade-offs for being loved and cared for.

Don't sweat the fact that sometimes you must do things that you'd rather not do.

This happens to be true for everybody, not just for kids. Get used to it. It's good practice for life. Keep a positive attitude. Whenever your parents' views are contrary to yours and you find yourself having to do something that you'd rather not do, ask yourself, *is it really that bad?* Chances are very good that if you can put whatever it is into the proper perspective, that it really isn't that bad.

Never lose sight of the fact that your parents love you and want what is best for you. Focus on this reality makes it a lot easier to see things from your parents' point of view. Try to imagine yourself in their place. You have asked your son or daughter to choose more appropriate friends. The ones with whom he or she currently associates are constantly getting in trouble at school. You're at the mall one day and you see a couple of them being arrested for shoplifting. Right away you think about your child and send up a silent prayer that your child is at school. *Why aren't Marty and Jasmine at school?* You immediately ask yourself. *I wonder if their parents know they're at the mall.*

If you are able to put yourself in your parents' place sometimes and visualize what it must be like to have your child constantly challenge your authority, this occasional reality check can serve to help you to realize that it really isn't that bad; that obeying one's parents is not something a kid ought to sweat, it's something a kid ought to expect to have to do. So don't sweat it, just do it, and you will be a happier, less frazzled young person.

27.

Cigarettes

There are some lines you shouldn't even go near, let alone cross. Cigarettes are one of these lines. Nobody is born addicted to cigarettes. And that's where *not going near* certain lines enters the picture. You see, a smart young person will not even *try* a cigarette. A savvy young person will recognize that anyone who offers a cigarette is no friend.

It is no secret that cigarettes are lethal. In years past, many people were addicted to cigarettes long before they knew that their addiction could kill them. No one can claim lack of knowledge any longer as a reason for his or her addiction to cigarettes. There are no acceptable excuses for putting a cigarette to your lips and lighting up.

It is against the law for you to even purchase cigarettes. Don't sweat it if some of your peers are less intelligent than you and are willing to demonstrate this by smoking cigarettes. This does not mean that you are less cool or that they are more cool. What it really means is that they are willing to risk an early death for the sake of appearing cool. Do not risk your health for the sake of a cigarette. You might have no intention of getting hooked. The reality is that there are many cigarette addicts who would tell you that they began smoking because they thought it was cool. But they can't tell you. They are now dead of lung cancer and other cigarette-smoking related diseases. Don't sweat it, just don't risk it!

28.

Say No to Drugs

Another of those lines that you shouldn't even go near is drugs. If anybody offers you drugs, give him a resounding *NO!* Then recognize that this person is not a friend even though he may appear friendly. Learn to discern the difference between being friendly and being a friend. Anybody can appear friendly in order to obtain a desired end, but a real friend will be supportive of the goals you have for yourself.

Nobody aspires to be a drug addict. Addiction makes sneak attacks. It has a way of sneaking up on people who are foolish enough to experiment with drugs. Remember: there are some lines you shouldn't even go near, let alone cross. Don't even go near *drugs*. Don't sweat it if someone calls you nerdy or some other foolish name that does not describe you. Know yourself and you will not be intimidated by people who call you names because you refuse to allow yourself to get involved with drugs. It's one of the smartest decisions you will ever make for yourself. Drugs are nothing to play with. *Don't play with them*. Don't associate with other young people who involve themselves with drugs.

If you know or learn that some of your peers are experimenting with drugs, you are obligated to tell someone in authority, even if you feel that you must do it anonymously. Don't sweat it that you are telling on your peers or friends. You will be helping them, though they will probably not view this reality as the fact that it is in their current state of mind. Keep in mind that you are responsible for the choices that you make. Make the choice not to get involved with drugs. Clearly it is a wise choice!

29.

Your Room, Your Space

You love your room. It's your space. It's the one place in the house where you can be the boss. Well, it did used to be that way, but since you are now responsible for picking up behind yourself and for keeping your room straight, it now seems that every time you turn around, your mom is on your back about your messy room.

If it's my room, why can't I keep it like I like it? You often ask yourself. Step back to gain a little perspective. Think about it. It is your room, but your room is part of the family's home. Try to get *the big picture.* Try to see things from your mom's perspective. There are some very important reasons why she wants you to keep your room less messy. First and foremost, she is responsible for teaching you about orderliness. If she doesn't, who will? Chances are excellent that if your parents do not teach you about keeping some order in your personal space, you will never learn to do so. And admit it: you don't really like your room messy, you just don't want to have to exert the effort that it will take to keep your room neat. You love your room when your mom *breaks down* and gives it a thorough cleaning.

Your parents have asked you not to take food into your room. *If it's my room, why can't I eat in it sometimes?* You have, no doubt, asked yourself this question on more than one occasion. Again it is necessary for you to look at the *bigger picture*. Think about it for a few minutes. Admit that there have been times when you were told to clean your room. Your mom looks in hours later and the room appears perfectly neat. But upon closer inspection, she discovers that most of the clutter has been shoved into the closet and under the bed.

Now, mentally add bits of uneaten food to this stuff that has been shoved under the bed or into the closet, and it becomes perfectly clear why food in your room is not a good idea.

Don't sweat it that you can't eat in your room or that your parents expect you to keep your room less messy. Acknowledge that your parents know best. Accept that there are times when they have your best interest at heart, even when you do not agree with nor understand their requests. Don't sweat it, just do it.

30.

On Homework

Some kids don't have any problems with homework. They have specific times each day set aside to do their homework. Homework has become a regular part of their routine and they don't sweat it. They just settle down at the kitchen table or at the desk in their room, or in some other convenient place, and get it done. If you are one of these kids, congratulations! This section isn't for you.

But if you are one of the kids who always

has good intentions but no homework when you show up in the class for which the homework was assigned, read on.

You don't have to continue to sweat doing homework. You can make it a part of your routine, but *you* and *only you* can make it that. **Here's how**:

-Write down each homework assignment, preferably in a homework assignment tablet (loose-leaf paper gets lost).

-Set aside a specific time each day just for homework. If you have no assigned homework, keep this specific time a part of your routine by reading from a good book.

-Keep school supplies in a specific place so that when you are ready to do your homework, you won't have the excuse of having to run around looking for supplies.

-**H**onor the specific homework time. Turn off the television, radio and other distractions. If you can't do this because others are watching or listening, remove yourself from the room where the distractions are taking place.

Do this for two weeks, without fail, and homework will become a part of your regular routine.

Recall that there are some decisions that no one can make for you but you. Creating a helpful routine for yourself is one of those decisions. You do not have to sweat homework. As an intelligent young person who is a student in school, you know that you should expect to have homework. In fact, something would be amiss if you didn't have any homework assigned. *Admit this, if only to yourself!* Only you can make the determination to let your efforts rise above your excuses, so don't sweat it, just do it!

31.

He Said/She Said

How many times have you allowed *he said* or *she said* to cause you problems? Don't answer that, just think about it. Now recognize that you don't have to get *caught up* in the *he said/she said* controversies in your environment. You can demonstrate by your response or lack of response, that you are not interested in what *he* or *she* said.

Sean tells Jewel that Sara said that she is *loose*. Jewel confronts Sara. Sara tells Jewel that she didn't say that; Sue is the one who said it. Jewel confronts Sue. Sue becomes infuriated. "What right have you to come in my face with that?" she demands.

A loud, disruptive screaming match takes place in the hallway as students are changing classes. This controversy results from *he said/she said*. The principal summons both Jewel and Sue to his office.

"What are you two thinking about disrupting this school like that? I should rephrase that question since obviously you weren't thinking, neither of you! I know your parents do not approve of this kind of behavior," he says. "They will be informed!"

They begin to explain to him the *he said, she said stuff*. The principal tells them that he has already addressed this topic in the meeting that was held with students right after school started and that he doesn't want to know what *he or she said*. He explains to them that ignoring *he said/she said* type comments can help them to avoid these types of problems. "If you had followed my advice, you wouldn't be in this predicament right now," he tells them.

Both girls are assigned *in-school suspension*. Both girls must take referral notices home to their parents. At home each is put on punishment, all because of *he said/she said*. Do not allow yourself to get caught up in this type of controversy. Don't sweat *he said/she said*. Ignore it.

32.

Don't Text While Driving

Remember our earlier discussion about determination? Well, determination is the main ingredient in *the winner's recipe*. It is the first step on the journey to success. Whatever your goal, whether short-term or long-term, in order to achieve it, you must first determine to do so.

Make the decision that you will not text while driving. It involves a mindset.

That's the easy part. Next comes *the not so easy part*: the determination that you won't sweat it that many of your friends do so. **R**emember: you are not responsible for the decisions your friends make, but you are responsible for the ones that you make.

No doubt you have heard and may even know someone who lost his or her life texting while driving or caused others to lose their lives. Don't place yourself in this precarious position. There is nothing any more important than preserving your own life; nothing more important than taking care of yourself. You can do that only if you are willing to delay gratification, and in this situation, doing so may very well save your life and the lives of others.

Don't sweat it that you have friends who say they text all the time while driving. You're intelligent. You know that you can't look at the texting screen and at the road simultaneously! Use your intelligence for more than good grades. Use it to make wise decisions. Refusing to text while driving is one wise decision that could save your life and the lives of others.

Like all of your decisions, this is one only you can make. Think about it for a few moments and you will realize that no text is so important that it demands an immediate response, and even if it is, intelligence demands that you stop in a safe place (not on the side of the road) and respond to it.

Don't sweat it that you are the only one of your friends who refuses to text while driving. You know that it's dangerous to do so. Make the decision that you won't do it, and then just don't do it!

33.

Keep Your Opinions to Yourself

Sometimes it might be a difficult thing to do, but with practice, anything becomes easier. One of the things you need to learn to do is to keep your opinions to yourself. Don't sweat it that there will be times when you want to express your opinion but it is not appropriate to do so. Guess what? This happens to be true for every one of us.

"But everyone is entitled to his or her opinion," you say. And you are completely correct. But being entitled to an opinion is not the same thing as being entitled to express an opinion. Say, for example, that Becky's opinion is that you are ugly. She is entitled to that opinion, but she isn't entitled to hurt your feelings or to embarrass you by saying that to you. And while you might be thinking, *I don't care what Becky thinks*, once Becky says the words, they are no longer just her thoughts.

It is extremely important that you accept as part of your reality that you do not have the right to say hurtful or embarrassing things to other people. Just as everybody else is, you are entitled to your opinion always, but you are not always entitled to express your opinion, and neither is anybody else.

Acceptance of the reality that you are not always entitled to the expression of your opinion can save you a lot of headaches as well as a lot of heartaches. Do not sweat it if, from time to time, you encounter others who behave as if they are not aware that there are times when their best interests will be served by keeping their opinions to themselves. You *do not* have to follow their lead. Think before you express your opinion. Ask yourself: *Is my opinion helpful or hurtful? Would I appreciate hearing someone else express a like or similar opinion about me? Will the expression of my opinion generate feelings of goodwill or animosity?* Answer these questions honestly before you decide whether or not to express your opinion, and you will be a happier, well-liked young person.

Continue reading 32 other topics in *Hang In There, Kid,* which is the second book in this 3-part series. *Just Do It, Kid,* which is the third book in this series focuses on 36 additional topics. They are both available on Amazon and Amazon Kindle.

I hope reading this series of books will help you make smart decisions when faced with life's hardest questions.

Glossary of Terms

acknowledge: *admit; concede*

adolescence: *teen years; youth*

advantage: *good; improvement*

allegiance: *devotion; loyalty*

alternate: *every other*

alternative: *option; choice*

anonymously: *unnamed*

apologetic: *expressing regret; sorry*

application: *a request, as for employment*

appointment: *meeting*

appropriate: *suitable; befitting*

articulate: *utter; well-spoken*

aspire: *strive*

attitude: *disposition; feeling*

avail: *help; assistance*

axiom: *maxim; cliché*

catalyst: *reactor; matter*

compassion: *kindness; feeling*

complicated: *difficult; complex*

connotation: *implied meaning; essence*

consideration: *thoughtfulness; attention*

controversial: *arguable; subject to start an argument*

cop out: (slang): *give up; quit*

corporation: *company; business*

counterproductive: *disadvantageous; unfavorable*

cram: *crowd; ram; pack*

cultivate: *enlighten; humanize*

definitely: *certainly; surely*

deliberately: *consciously; willfully*

destination: *goal; target*

destiny: *future; fortune*

determination: *resolve*

discern: *determine; notice*

disharmony: *discord*

disparaging: *complaining; critical*

disruption: *disturbance; disorder*

distraction: *confusion; diversion*

dividend: pay off; return

elusive: seemingly deceptive

embarrassment: discomfort; unease

encounter: meeting

endeavor: try; effort

enlist: enroll in the armed forces

entitled: permitted; allowed

equitable: fair; just

eventually: as time goes by

fleeting: passing quickly; brief

flexibility: versatility; ability to bend

foundation: groundwork; basis

frazzled: (slang): bothered; upset; torn

frustration: feeling of disappointment; anger at defeat

gauging: measuring

generate: make or produce; create

harmoniously: agreeably; peaceably

hassle: harass; bother

initial: first

insubordination: disobedience; defiance

insurmountable: *impossible; hopeless*

integer: *whole number*

intimidate: *scare; discourage*

lethal: *deadly; fatal*

loose: *immoral; easy*

maintain: *keep up; continue*

military: *armed forces*

mutual: *shared; reciprocal*

mythological: *fabled; legendary*

necessarily: *certainly; fundamentally*

negative: *disapproving; contrary*

numerous: *many; abundant*

obstinate: *stubborn; inflexible*

opportunity: *chance*

option: *choice; alternative*

perseverance: *determination; tenacity*

perspective: *viewpoint; bias*

pledge: *promise*

Pocahontas : *a popular, animated movie title*

point of view: *position; viewpoint*

positive: *absolute; certain*

potentially: *probably*

predicament: *dilemma*

predict: *foretell; guess*

productive: *fruitful; generative*

provoke: *anger; incite*

random: *chance; hit-or-miss*

recruit: *enroll in the armed forces*

relevance: *pertinence; significance*

resolve: *determine; will*

resounding: *loud; reverberating*

restriction: *restraint; limitation*

retaliate: *avenge; repay*

scholarship: *financial aid awarded to a student*

sibling: *brother; sister*

snide remarks: *nasty words*

substantial: *abundant; important*

summon: *call; invite*

supportive: *encouraging; offering moral support*

suspicious: *questionable; doubtful*

sympathetic: *kind; considerate; sensitive*

tattletale: (slang) *informer; busybody*

temporary: *passing; transitory*

unintentional: *accidental; unplanned*

unoccupied: *empty; vacant*

verbal: *spoken; stated*

vicinity: *nearness; surrounding*

visitation : *going there; stay*

Use the space below if you have ideas and comments for additional topics you would like to have covered in a fourth volume of the *Don't Sweat It, Kid Series.*

_____ *'s Ideas and Comments*

(Your Name)

1. _____
2. _____
3. _____
4. _____
5. _____
6. _____
7. _____
8. _____
9. _____
10. _____

About the Author

The author, Joyce Willard Teal, is a graduate of Prairie View A & M University. She is an award-winning teacher in the Dallas Independent School District. She has taught school in Dallas for the past four years, but her career path has taken her through New Jersey, Maryland, Pennsylvania, Georgia and Virginia, where she taught boys and girls in the public schools of these states.

Dr. Teal is the 1998 recipient of the *Excellence in Teaching Award.* This award is sponsored by *Shell Oil Company* for the *National Council of Negro Women.* It is a prestigious award presented annually to a select few in the teaching profession.

In addition to teaching and writing professionally, Dr. Teal is an inspirational speaker, guest lecturer and storyteller. She also conducts workshops based on her book, *Sister, It's Not Okay* and a 3-day workshop session for youth based on this book, *Don't Sweat It, Kid.* In order to schedule workshops or speaking engagements, you can contact Dr. Teal through REBAssociates Resource Network International at (301) 420-0000

Other Books by Dr. Teal:

Don't Sweat It, Kid-- **Book 1 in this 3-part series** (available on Amazon Kindle)

Hang in There, Kid – Book 2 (available on Amazon Kindle)

Just Do It, Kid — **Book 3 in this 3-part series** (available on Amazon Kindle)

It's Okay to be Different

The Yield

Sister, It's Not Okay

Young Sister, It's Not Okay

The Point System

A.E.P.

MotorVation

A Product of His Grace (Poems of Praise)

Are You Raising One of the Next Generation of Hoodlums?

The Tree That Tells a Tale

Learning A,B,C's with Seth

Learning 1,2,3's with Seth and Friends

If you would like information regarding Dr. Joyce Willard Teal speaking at your event, please write to:

REBAssociates Resource Network International

Attention: **Reba N. Burruss-Barnes**,

Publicist

2312 Brooks Dr. #202

Suitland, MD 20746-1014

Call

(301) 420-0000

or

e-mail rebabarnes@aol.com

40235843R00094

Made in the USA
Charleston, SC
28 March 2015